How to Buy and Sell a Home, and Everything In Between

ROBERT DESBRUSLAIS

Book design by Publishing Push

Paperback ISBN: 978-1-80227-041-9
eBook ISBN: 978-1-80227-042-6

Published by PublishingPush.com

Contents

A word from the Author

As a Building Surveyor and Member of the RICS since 1986, I have been involved in the increasingly frantic residential property industry for over 30 years.

During that period, I have inspected thousands of homes and acted for hundreds of clients from first-time buyers of a modest studio flat in Crawley, to buying agents and solicitors representing the superrich purchasing multimillion pound town houses in Belgravia. Rarely a day goes by without me talking to at least one, and usually several professionals in the industry, from solicitors, estate agents, developers, mortgage brokers and financial advisers, somewhat trendily now described as wealth managers. Most days I talk to purchasers and sellers, who can be anyone from an excited first-time buyer to a concerned elderly widow moving for the first time in many years, and the hundreds of others in between.

I have seen the market rise inexorably during this time, with just the occasional so called crash (in hindsight, merely a blip), and watched many a person make fortunes simply by moving from one home to another, while others have lost out on their dream homes, often simply due to indecision.

I have seen people in tears, angry and ecstatic. I have watched, listened and learned. It seemed only right to put it all down on paper.

Introduction

'Oh my God!'

These are not words that I would normally blurt out loud in front of a home owner when carrying out an survey of their house, but on this occasion, I just couldn't stop myself.

Admittedly the phase is one I often mutter *quietly* under my breath, and with some justification. You name it, from squalor, filth and stink to incredible splendour and outrageous décor - after years of surveying homes, I have seen it. I have been bitten by dogs (three times, once in a school I was surveying), asked to hold a baby, propositioned by a vendor (that survey ended very quickly), and just when I thought I *had* seen it all, the other day I surveyed a house where the two deceased vendors were in a burial ground - in the garden. Needless to say, the executors of the sale had cordoned off that section of the garden so it was not included in the sale as they thought some buyers might otherwise be put off.....

Anyway, usually my verbal editor reflex is quick enough to stop my mouth. On the occasion I am about to describe, however, it just slipped out. In fact I tell a lie, I didn't say *'oh my god'*, the phrase was a little more direct, and not to be repeated here.

The sweet elderly owner of the house came rushing into the living room from the kitchen where she was kindly making me a cup of tea. In the meantime, her dog, an excitable miniature poodle, in fact excitable is a categoric understatement, he had spent the entire five minutes since I arrived yapping at my ankles. As always on such occasions, and having been bitten three times, I had chosen to ignore the pooch, they soon lose interest if you feign a lack of it.

This little chap, however, it seems was somewhat of an exception. In fact so overcome was he by my presence, that he had created an exceptionally large poo (well, exceptionally large for an exceptionally small dog) in the middle of the living room carpet. During my attempts to ignore him I had spent most of the time staring, as surveyors do, at the walls, the ceilings , the doors, windows and so on. It was only when I looked at the floor and risked eye contact with my new canine friend that the unsettling discovery was made.

This, however, was not the reason for the blurted out expletive.

Unbeknown to me, while wandering round the room, I had succeeded in treading the said poo throughout the living room carpet. To make matters worse, the carpet was one of white woollen (actually probably Nylon) deep pile opulence, which until now, had been as pure as the driven snow.

This unfortunate occurrence happened many years ago while carrying out a valuation (by the way, a valuation is not a survey, see chapter 8), on this elderly lady's house in her latest attempt to sell what had been her beloved home for the past 25 years. She was at the same time, upset, embarrassed and clearly angry, thankfully her pet, not at me.

This episode might seem minor in the bigger context of selling a house, but such an event is often the straw that breaks the camel's back during the stress of selling your home.

The lovely lady (Margaret – not her real name obviously) and I suddenly had a mutual bond, initially borne in embarrassment, but which inevitably led to a prolonged conversation over tea not just about this unfortunate event, but more importantly, the apparent tortuously convoluted process that is buying and selling a home in the UK. Margaret was a widow on her own with little help from relatives and felt somewhat at the mercy of the only people she knew that could help - her estate agents.

Yes, you read correctly. All her support came from her estate agent.

Don't get me wrong, estate agents do an excellent job and despite the public's perception, have to work hard for their fee (in fact, in most cases they do not get paid at all if they don't sell your home), but they are not the most impartial of advisers when you are selling what is probably your most precious asset, and navigating your way through the home buying maze.

To make matters worse, Margaret's house was under offer, but she had not yet found anywhere to move, so felt under pressure and was beginning to panic.

So I explained to Margaret why actually this should not be so stressful, that she was in control, and what next steps she could take in her search for a home and to prepare for her move. After all, I have spoken to enough people about it over the years, and learned an enormous amount.

Not only did she feel better, but she also said, 'You should write a book on this!'

Don't be daft, I said, I've got no time for that..............

The property obsession

For decades, and especially since the Thatcher era, people of the UK have been obsessed with property ownership.

Around dinner tables up and down the country, rarely does an evening pass without a discussion about property ownership and house prices. It seems every other day one can open a newspaper and see the tabloids screaming 'home owners earning £500 a month for doing nothing', or conversely 'home owners losing £1000 a week as house prices crash!'.

It is hardly surprising that the subject of property ownership and house prices is so often on the forefront of our minds.

For some, the idea of owning their own home may seem a pipe dream and others simply find the commitment too frightening. Most, however, after the initial fear and obstacles, adapt to property ownership like a duck to water.

Nearly everyone, it seems, wants to be a home owner.

About this Book

It is well-known cliché but also a fact; buying a home is without doubt the biggest financial decision we make. It may not be the biggest purchase you ever make, after all some successful people spend more money on art and cars than they do on houses, but it is the financial commitment of your first home purchase that is so defining. Once the decision is made, rarely do people look back. Invariably we sell the first house and buy a bigger one. Then throughout our life we move several times as we encounter various stages of life: the first steps to independence, relationships, children, relocation, divorce (sadly today a very common cause of house sales and purchases) and so on. Invariably once you are on the ladder, these events all touch our decisions along the housing ladder. Even after we die we have an impact on the property market; invariably our house has to be sold or given to others as part of our estate.

Despite the sheer scale and complexity of the British property market there is no guide or 'bible' for those with limited experience in making such an important purchase. It is not just the first time buyer that is daunted; some long-term owners may not have moved for decades. Often I encounter home owners that are downsizing after the children have left the roost and have completely forgotten just how complex and infuriating the process can be.

This book is intended for anyone involved in the business of buying or selling their home, but especially for first time buyers and those owners that have not sold or bought a home for years. Both face the same challenges and uncertainty. Many long term owners believe the property market is unrecognisable from the form it took when they last moved. In fact, this is far from the case and the process remains surprisingly familiar; the prices and taxes have changed but the challenges remain the same.

In this book, I hope to share with you my experiences, the experience of others involved in property ownership and provide you with a guide on how to buy and sell property and the challenges you are likely to encounter on the way. It could be the home of your dreams, or the first of many purchases as you climb the property ladder. In fact, this book might help you decide if you should buy a house at all, after all, property ownership is not for everyone. In my experience, however, these individuals are the exception and very often at some stage in their life, they decide that, after all, owning a home is a good idea.

Of course you might read this book simply to either reinforce your opinion on homeownership, or for the sheer entertainment. I would be extremely pleased in the case of the latter and hopefully some of the anecdotes will make this not only an informative read, but also an enjoyable one.

If you are buying your first home, or making the leap after many years of owning the same home, good luck, your adventure starts here.......

CHAPTER 1

To Buy or Not to Buy, to Sell or Not to Sell?

In 1984, I bought my first home. I was a student, and my wife was a secretary. We obtained a 95% mortgage from the Burgess Hill Building Society, astonishingly, based purely on a multiple of my wife's secretarial salary. What is even more incredible, is this property was not in some quite backwater with no access to even a decent pub and curry house; it was a one bedroom garden flat in East Dulwich, London. Okay, at the time East Dulwich was not the salubrious area it is today, but it was still in the most expensive city in the UK, in fact, one of the most expensive cities in the world.

It was not too difficult to save up for the deposit, obtain a mortgage and 'abracadabra!' - we were homeowners.

How times have changed.

Today, you would need a salary approaching £100,000 to buy that very same flat. Do you know a secretary that earns anything like that sum? I certainly don't. Ok, maybe the Secretary of State.

Back then, affordability meant the decision to buy a home was a no-brainer and in hindsight (yes, it's a wonderful thing) it is surprising just how few of our contemporaries were prepared to take the leap, or had even considered it for that matter. Even in those times of incredible affordability, agonising over homeownership and the associated commitment was the norm. For anyone who did commit in those times of true affordability, and stayed 'in the game', the relentless rise of property prices has made them a member of an exclusive club; a fortunate generation of home owners with average salaries yet bags of equity in their property. Some are now members of an elite group of property millionaires, and many have taken the opportunity to reinvest in other property to help fund their retirement.

Today people look back with affection and envy at those times of incredible affordability, yet far from thinking they have missed the boat, demand is greater now than ever before; we just cannot get enough of home ownership and property investment.

As a rule, those who want to buy a home remain committed to doing so regardless of affordability. However, for those who are uncertain, prices are the main deterrent, but history tells us that this is not a reason to delay buying unless there is absolutely no way of raising the money. Raising the money is however invariably easier than it may at first seem.

In the meantime, what other factors are there to consider? Before asking yourself this question, you really need to delve a little deeper; do you actually *want* to buy a home?

When I started this chapter I was thinking about how to convince you that property ownership is the way forward for all and then it occurred to me; I might be wasting my time and yours. If you are reading this book, I doubt it is because you don't want to buy. If you are reading for entertainment then fair play and thank you, but you might want to swap it for Lord of the Rings, which does not guide you through the labyrinth that is the property market, but is similarly complex.

If simply you just do not know whether to buy on not, I give you the following advice (for those of you that want to crack on, this is brief).

Here are some of the more common and obscure reasons I have been given as to why people do not own their own home.

• I don't believe in owning possessions.

Fair enough, in fact this is a belief of one of my friends, and an honourable if difficult life to follow in this modern age (if this is you, I hope you were given this book and did not buy it because that would be counter to your principles. Unless of course you give it so someone else, preferably a person that is desperate to buy).

- Death.

  Buying a property without doubt will not benefit you. However, pending death is not necessarily a reason not to buy property if you want to look after your loved ones.

- I don't want commitment.

  A common quandary, especially for younger people. Owning a property however does not have to hold back the adventurer, and may even be a great base and income earner to facilitate your lifestyle. Of course if like Elon Musk you plan to live the rest of your life on Mars (he's serious), it will probably be quite difficult to manage your property portfolio while bouncing around the red planet a few hundred thousand miles away. Mind you, if you can get to Mars there probably is no affordability barrier, and it could be a good time to buy there…...

- I can't be bothered.

  Many people don't buy or move because frankly they're too lazy to bother. If that's the case, it probably means you are happy where you are, but do you really want to be in that rented one bedroom flat in 10 years' time?

  There is of course one advantage in being lazy. It usually means you are good at delegation and getting other people to do stuff. I wouldn't describe myself as lazy (better double check that line with my wife) but doing stuff you do not enjoy is a bit of a waste of your life. For example, the admin of my business would be left in an untidy pile of crumpled paper and bills if I took total responsibility for it. So I give all to somebody else who is organised, better and quicker at it, leaving me to the activities I enjoy; playing music, surveying (seriously) and yes, writing this book.

So maybe laziness is the wrong word. You can be lazy *and* proactive, and with a bit of positive thinking, you can own the home of your dreams.

• Prices Might Fall

Correct, they might. However, do we worry about this when we buy anything else that we use and need? New cars devalue the moment they are driven out of the car dealers garage and in time are often scrapped. Expensive meals are worth nothing at the end of the evening. Apart from intentional investments and perhaps the odd lucky buy, virtually everything we buy devalues and eventually becomes worthless. No one complains about it though, we just expect it. When was the last time you heard someone say, 'I can't believe no-one wants to but by my 10 year old worn out handmade suit for more than I bought it for!'?

Yet the thought of a house losing value puts the fear of god into even the most rational potential property owner. So why is this? The reason is quite simple. The remorseless rise of property prices has confused the general public in to thinking home ownership is an investment. Unless you are a professional property investor, it is not – it is a home; *your* home. A home is something we yearn for, it doesn't have to make money, just look at the thousands of people that spend years in rented property and spend thousands making it their space. It just happens that owning a home has a far greater chance of growing in value then that collection of posh suits.

There is also another huge benefit; instead of paying rent to someone else, you pay down your mortgage! Even if the house *never* goes up in value, when the mortgage is paid, you own it, and it has value. If you continue to rent, you are paying the home owners mortgage for them and after 25 years own nothing but the furniture.

- International disaster. A pandemic, for example.

  Well, contrary to all economic forecasts at the start of the awful COVID 19 pandemic in early 2020, the house market has not imploded, it has positively exploded. The reasons are many, and there is no sign of a let up.

- I don't have any money.

  Well I guess that does make life difficult, but there are solutions!

Of course there is one overarching deterrent that encompasses many of the above:

Fear.

Don't worry, read on, we can overcome!

Chapter Summary

- Decide, is property ownership for me?
- If not, are you really just making excuses?
- If you 'play safe' and just rent, the money is simply paying off the landlord's mortgage and you still have nothing.
- When you buy a home, once you pay of the mortgage you have an asset, even if prices fall.

CHAPTER 2

Overcoming Fear and Taking the Leap

If you are looking yearningly at property ownership, or if you own your home and would love to move, fear will often stop you in your tracks. Fear has a paralysing effect on decision-making. Fear causes persistent procrastination, and big decisions are hidden under a pile of inconsequential social media, binge watching and sock sorting.

The fear factor holds us all back at times and suspends our progress through life. Almost without exception, however, making a hard life decision is far easier than expected and has huge positive implications. How often have you thought, 'Oh no I'm really not looking forward to seeing the boss...' and left realising it was an easy encounter? Even when a decision does create aggravation, invariably inconvenience is short lived but the benefits can be enormous, even life changing.

So decide one way or the other; either don't do it or get on with it. Procrastination simply fills your mind with fog, and the indecision will probably mean wasted opportunities. If you make a conscious decision not to buy you are released from the paralysis of indecision. You can do something else exciting. Buy a car. Go travelling. Buy an expensive guitar (that's my favourite). But make the decision and do something else.

If you decide to buy (or move if you already own) then who knows what lies ahead? Believe me it won't be boring.

By now you will have realised that I don't really think anybody should decide *not* to buy a home. I'm not saying we should all become property magnets or even small-time landlords. Nothing however, beats the feeling of owning your own home, and never again having to worry that your landlord will return from Australia and want *their* home back......

So let's overcome the fear by taking things one step at a time.

CHAPTER 3

Affordability and Getting a Mortgage

So where should you start? There is one simple answer, especially if you are entirely new to the market or have not moved for years.

Find out what you can afford.

You need to work out your absolute maximum price limit. If you are a cash buyer, this is usually a relatively straight forward question.

If however you are not, affordability is a little more complex and what you can buy hinges on how much you can borrow. This depends on various factors, but predominantly your income, savings (if you have any) and how the lender views your spending habits.

Now you probably think you know how much or little you earn and are worth, and what you can afford, but might be surprised to find out the reality is somewhat different. You need an expert assessment. If you do not already have a competent financial adviser, then get one. They will look at your entire financial situation and could find ways of improving your affordability. This might mean giving up a few luxuries, even if just on a temporary basis. for example, subscriptions and gym memberships. Put simply, the less outgoings you have, the more they are likely to lend you.

More importantly, make sure you pay all bills on time and do not exceed credit card limits. If the bank thinks you have little control on your spending habits, they will not look favourably on lending you a shed load for a house.

Next, find a mortgage broker. The financial adviser and mortgage broker may in fact be in the same but I would advise against an individual that does both, ideally you need someone that specialises in mortgage work.

Choosing the right mortgage broker is not an entirely simple matter. There are three classes regulated by the Financial Conduct Authority (FCA). Each differs on the range of deals they can access and consequently, the scope of advice they are able to offer (sorry if this is a little dry, I know I said buying a house is exciting but boring bits are difficult to avoid….).

These include:

- Tied mortgage brokers. They offer mortgage products available from a single lender – probably not a good option.

- Multi-tied mortgage brokers – they have access to products from a select panel of lenders. Better but you could miss out on good deals they cannot access, but sometimes they will access preferential rates.

- Whole of market brokers – they have access to all the mortgage products made available to mortgage brokers. This is usually the best option as they are free to find the best deal by comparing a much wider range of products and lenders.

If you are not sure which category the broker you approach falls in, just ask.

Once you have your chosen advisers, they will give you a reasonable estimate of how much you can afford before the application is made. This will require accurate information from you upfront, details of your salary, bonuses and any other income, the maximum deposit you can afford etc. Armed with this information they will go out into the market and find the best deal available to you. In other words, they will do the donkey work for you.

Of course you could apply to various banks yourselves, and save the brokerage fee (an independent mortgage broker does not come free, but a good one is worth every penny). The chances are however, you will spend most evenings filling lengthy forms online for each lender, when you could be doing something far better with your precious free time. Better to fill in just one form, hand it to the expert and let them do the rest. In fact, if you search the market yourself, the chances are you will miss the best deal available.

Again, being lazy can pay.

Mortgage lenders do have a habit of changing the goalposts regularly so be prepared to accept that the deal a broker may have in mind for you might not be available by the time you are in a position to purchase.

Indeed, this has happened to me in the past. My wife and I accepted a mortgage offer on a house we were purchasing, but after numerous delays, the offer had nearly run out. However, in that time our mortgage broker discovered the same lender had come up with a better deal so that on that occasion the delay worked out in our favour. We were lucky; often the reverse is true.

No need for a mortgage?

At the opposite end of the scale, if you are downsizing and own your home outright, answering the question of affordability can still be complicated and depends on other income and savings you have. If most of your money is tied up in the property, you must decide what you want left after selling up and buying another property. Perhaps you want a few well-earned trips around the world and just a bolthole in the UK. Alternatively, you might want a home you never have to leave. I would advise against selling and going in to rented accommodation; you will visibly see your nest egg disappear before your eyes.

Getting a mortgage.

Unfortunately, it is harder now to get a mortgage than in the late 90s and early noughties. Back then, virtually anyone could get a 'sub-prime mortgage'. You could virtually make up how much you earned and provided there was a 15% deposit, the world was your oyster.

It all seemed such a grand idea at the time, but the sub-prime mortgage created one of the greatest financial calamities western economies have faced. Tell someone they can borrow what they want based on a multiple of a salary that they can make up then human nature kicks in and they will borrow too much.

Developers especially loved the scheme and created a buying frenzy by offering people cash back after they purchased. In effect, you could buy a flat for say £250,000 (just below the 3% stamp duty of the time – an explanation of Stamp Duty is provided later in this chapter), borrow 85%, i.e. £212,500 based on a fictitious income, and on completion of the purchase, the developer would give you the deposit back. Many people thought they had won the lottery and some even purchased several flats on Buy to Let schemes without having the shell out a penny.

As they say, however, there is no such thing as a free lunch.

When did you ever meet a developer that sold a flat below market value? In fact new build housing is without exception more expensive than the second-hand equivalent, and with some justification, everything is, well, new, but as soon as you buy, the home is second hand. Those homes marketed for £250,000 with a cash back of £37,500 were probably worth about £200,000 on the second-hand market. The developers were knocking out hundreds of flats and selling them to hapless buyers instantly lumbered with negative equity (negative equity is where the value of your property is less than your mortgage loan). The biggest winners? The packaging mortgage brokers. They received enormous introduction fees from the sub-prime lenders, *and* were permitted to instruct independent surveyors to carry out the mortgage valuations. If the valuers did not play the game and value the properties at the stated price, in this example, £250,000, the brokers would stop giving them the business; just a little conflict in interest there! The sub-prime lenders then sold their mortgage 'book' to the likes of the Halifax who ended up with a huge pile of debt that came crashing down on their head.

Once the stack of cards started to fall, so to did the value of the flats the duped buyers were desperate to sell. Consequently lots of wealthy cash rich investors hoovered up a stack pf bargains and prices soon bounced back. Ultimately, the lack of affordable housing stock prevents a prolonged crash in the market, especially in this country, but those behind the huge housing bubble ruined a lot of lives and have a lot to answer for.

There is another whole book I could write about that subject and you will find plenty of horror stories on the internet.

So yes it was easy to get a mortgage, but it was also easy to fall into the trap of unaffordability, negative equity and personal bankruptcy.

Today the banks simply will not allow you to borrow more than you can afford. So it is essential you ask a reputable mortgage broker to work out exactly what that figure is. Don't worry, the subprime brokers have all gone. The last one I spoke to now owns a sweet shop selling less risky treats, and another owns a string of kabab shops.

Another footnote regarding affordability - honesty pays.

The amount you can borrow depends on how much you earn and proof of income is required. This can be where some self-employed people come unstuck. If clever accounting shows your income lower than it is, you will pay less tax, but don't expect a decent mortgage offer. A few years back a friend of mine was hoping to buy a lovely three bed semi for about £350,000. The mortgage payments were well within their capability and considerably less than the rent they were paying to the landlord (which of course was paying *his* mortgage). However, both she and her partner are self-employed and at the time had, shall we say, a creative approach to book keeping. The tax man thought they earned very little. Unfortunately so too did the mortgage company, who will only look at the proof of income, and they could not borrow anywhere near the amount required despite in truth earning easily enough.

So if you are self-employed and want to buy a property, don't fiddle the books; it will come back to haunt you! It seems only the super-rich get away with that. In fact my friends subsequently changed their approach and have at last succeeded in purchasing a lovely home.

Alternatives to a standard mortgage.

There are other methods of raising money. Legal methods that is, there are plenty illegal but I will leave others to discuss those with you.

Buy-to-let

The amount you borrow for a buy-to-let mortgage is not dependent on your income, but on the rental value of the property. You can usually borrow up to 75%, some-times more, provided the monthly rent is at least around 130% of the mortgage. These figures can vary wildly, and obviously banks may be a little bit more cautious if they think interest rates are going to go up (which at the time of writing is highly unlikely). There are also quite hefty mortgage charges. This method is only suitable if you already own a property. You cannot get a buy-to-let mortgage if you don't already own a home as the banks will think you're trying to be clever and live in it yourself as you don't have the income to prove the level of mortgage required.

The reverse of a buy-to-let is, yes that's right, let-to buy. If you live in a house that is eminently rentable, you can get a buy-to-let mortgage on the one you already own, and use that money to buy a house for yourself. Hence let to buy.

So how would this benefit a first time buyer? Well you can obtain a buy to let mortgage jointly with an investor that already owns a property, for example, a relative. They need own only a very small proportion of the home you are buying. The property could be rented out, and then after the fixed term of the mortgage is over (usually a minimum of two years) you could revert to a normal mortgage and move in. If when you first buy the dwelling it needs refurbishment, the increase in value from modernising the property should help create the deposit you need to buy out your fellow investor, and even sell and buy elsewhere.

There are legal complications, and you should not proceed without appropriate professional advice from a mortgage broker and lawyer. Also, if you want a decent return on this process which initially *is* an investment, get advice on what is best to buy; just because it is nice doesn't mean it will give you a decent rental return.

Other cost considerations.

1. Stamp Duty

If you're a first-time buyer you have may have heard the words 'stamp duty' followed by some cussing, but never fully understood the implications. When buying a home, the reason for cussing becomes evident. In my mind they should rename it the 'that's messed up my calculations' tax. It can have a significant impact on your affordability.

Stamp duty is a tax payable to the Treasury (of course) and is calculated as a percentage of your purchase. The percentage rises as the price goes up until it becomes very steep indeed.

The government changes the duty periodically. Unsurprisingly, as yet stamp duty has not gone down, although there was a minor adjustment in favour of low to middle range prices fairly recently and a big change in favour of the first time buyer. There have also been whisperings that stamp duty might be transferred to the vendor, but this did not materialise in the last budget and is an unlikely change.

At the time of writing, the government has introduced a stamp duty holiday to support the house market during the pandemic. This has proved an expensive mistake, as the market was showing no signs of collapsing and, in fact, has performed well across all price ranges, especially at the higher end, where the duty holiday has little impact on the purchaser's finances. As the holiday is temporary, I have ignored this short-term aberration and set out the charges you will most likely experience as follows:

At the time of writing, as a buyer, this is how much money you will need to find:

Non-first time buyers:-

Up to £125,000 (£40,000 for second home), good news, you pay no stamp duty.

£125,001 to 250,000, 2% - OK, reasonably affordable.

250,001 to 925,000, 5% - Getting pricey.

£925001 to £1.5 million -10%. Ouch.

£1.5 million +12%. Come on, you can afford it.

First time buyers:-

Up to £300,000, no stamp duty.

Up to £500,000, no stamp duty on the first £300,000, stamp duty on the remaining £200,000.

Above £500,000, normal stamp duty applies.

The percentage is incremental, so on the positive side if you are buying for say £500,000, you don't pay any tax on the first £125000. However, your total tax bill will still be significant, in this example, £15,000, the cost of a decent kitchen.

If this is a second home, another 3% is payable, a big consideration for investors and holiday home buyers.

As things stand, stamp duty is without doubt one of the main affordability considerations for people that want to move. Since stamp duty increased significantly, it is not surprising that many people choose to spend the money on home improvements instead of moving.

Mortgage set up costs, survey and legal fees.

Choosing a solicitor for the conveyance and arranging a survey is discussed later, but the cost implications should be built in to your initial affordability considerations.

It is tempting to choose the cheapest, but as many have learned to their cost, the decision should not be based on fees alone.

The cost will usually depend on what you are buying. If it is a leasehold property, the chances are the legal fees will be a little more due to the additional layer of complexity for the solicitor to consider. If you want a decent solicitor and surveyor, you should allow at least £1500 in combined fees, and considerably more if you are lucky enough to buy a home in the pricier range.

Chapter Summary

- Find a financial adviser and mortgage broker
- Avoid approaching lenders yourself, you might miss out on a better deal that brokers will find.
- If you are downsizing, work out how much cash you want to free up first, then set your buying limit.
- Telling the taxman you have low income reduces your potential mortgage offer
- Buy to Let can be an option for a first time buyer if you buy jointly with someone that already owns.
- Work out buying costs when calculating afford-ability, including Stamp Duty, Legal and survey and mortgage set up fees.

CHAPTER 4

Your Dream Home .... and How to Avoid a Nightmare

Okay so you've worked out what you can afford, now what are you going to buy?

Regardless of whether you are a first-time buyer, upsizing, downsizing or an investor there is one key consideration - location.

The phrase location location location was coined many years ago and for a very good reason. Location is without doubt the most important factor when buying a home. My brother once described a nice house in a dodgy location as a banana in a cesspit. Frankly I am still not entirely sure what he meant, but you get the gist; that gorgeous AGA in the kitchen will not eliminate the smell of the neighbouring sewage farm. It might be you can afford that lovely picture postcard cottage, but if it is blighted by a huge pylon, you can guarantee it will be the first to fall in value in a recession and even in a good market will have a ceiling on value that cannot be reflected by any number of improvements.

Often I hear people say 'such and such a town' is now the place to buy, Newtown is up-and-coming, etc. etc. Please, ignore these ill-informed property 'experts'. In a normal or rapidly rising market, these misguided declarations are made on a regular basis. The places referred to do seem cheap. Believe me however, they are not. Once the market turns they invariably fall in value first and furthest.

Of course an individual's definition of a good or bad location will vary.

Take Hastings. Hastings is a lovely town and I have absolutely nothing against it, parts of it are very nice indeed and it is definitely worth a visit. It is just in the wrong place and for most people in the south, is a really difficult commute. However, on many occasion I have seen investors come unstuck because they bought there when everywhere else had become too expensive. I know investors that purchased in the mid-2000s and hold property that has only now returned to the values attained 10 years ago. If however, they had purchased in Hastings at the depths of the subsequent recession, they would be laughing all the way to the bank. In fact, Hastings really is a place to buy - in a recession.

Perhaps one day the transport links will improve. However, when you consider how expensive it is proving to build the new high speed rail link from London to the north of England, something tells me that a similar link between London and Hastings will not be coming any time soon.

Even big developers can make the same mistake. Newhaven, another cheaper town on the south coast, is a thriving port. That is most likely what it will always be. It is not a thriving residential yummy mummy hotspot. However, one developer in their wisdom decided to build a number of luxury flats along the estuary. Making the same mistake as the private buyer that thought a lovely wet room would magically remove the smell of the local battery chicken farm, these very nice new properties did not magically remove the industrial port and scrap metal piles on the opposite side of the water. In fact, subsequent to that development in the mid-2000s, Newhaven was chosen as the location for the main waste incinerator serving the south.

Unsurprisingly, the developer went pear shaped and once again, many of the people who did buy homes in that development during the madness of the subprime mortgage market were lumbered with properties they couldn't sell. Some remain in negative equity today.

That said, if you want to live in Hastings or Newhaven because that is where you want your home, forget the investment value, buy there anyway, they are great towns in their own right, just make sure you are astute with your choice.

Of course we all crave a bargain. You should however avoid anything in a poor location unless we are in the depths of a property recession. It might seem counter intuitive to buy in a poor location and in a recession, but often this is where the bargains lie; the upside is far greater than the potential fall. As Yaz once sung, the only way is up. I would however recommend this only if you intend to move as soon as the market picks up, and the ill-informed are suddenly once again suggesting this is the place to buy.

These are just a few examples of why location should be your main consideration. I am not suggesting you must only buy somewhere that is a trendy hot spot, as said many times in this book, a house is a home first and an investment second, and there are usually very good reasons to buy other that a hot location, close family for example, but do ensure you buy with your eyes open and be aware of the implications and hidden location hazards.

Here are a few examples of what to avoid:

1. Unwelcome Surprises

2. Neighbours

A few years back friend of mine purchased a very lovely Georgian terraced house in one of the finest roads in Brighton. The location, Brunswick Village conservation area, is in Hove 'actually'. This is a beautiful spot within a stone's throw of the beach and with great shops, cafes, nightlife and schools. Perfect.

What they did not find out until spending a few days in their new home, was that the house two doors away was a shelter for the homeless and destitute.

These unfortunate members of society spent a great deal of time congregating outside the shelter and adjoining homes and would often engage every passer by including my friend's children in conversation, and offer to share their Jack Daniels too.

This is of course an essential use of housing (there is another whole book to be written here on social housing, and the destruction of the housing market by Thatcherism, but don't get me started on that right now). There is no escaping the fact we live in an unequal society. However, even if you are heavily involved in social services, it is probably best to avoid buying a house next door to the office.

Another common complaint is noisy neighbours. If you have just got your three-month-old baby to sleep in your new home, the last thing you want is thumping drum and bass next door. Of course likewise, next door might not appreciate the sound of your yelling bundle of fun at 5 o'clock in the morning having just fallen asleep to the sound of their booming woofer, and I'm not talking about their Great Dane, another potential hazard.

To mitigate the risk of these unfortunate circumstances and to avoid the unexpected, I strongly recommend you revisit the location of your potential new home at different times during the day and night to find out just what activities you should expect.

Building work and development.

Picture the scene. You are just stirring from the first night of blissful sleep in your gorgeous chocolate box cottage with its beautiful views, inglenook fireplace and chalk paint finishes, expecting the blissful sound of chirping, only to jerk awake to the thunderous racket of a JCB.

Now of course your solicitor will have made enquiries to establish whether there are pending developments that might affect the area. This forms part of the property 'search' arranged by you conveyancer (for further explanation about a property search, see chapter 8). However, the search will not include land that has not been the subject of a planning application and is not earmarked for future development.

For example, it is possible that, after you have exchanged contracts, your neighbour may put in a planning application for the construction of a large extension, conversion of their house into flats, or even construction of a house in their garden that overlooks your bedroom.

The nightmare scenario would be the prospect of new housing directly in front of your view. This is a very real risk in a country with a chronic housing shortage. Local authorities are under extreme pressure to meet new build targets and are bombarded by developers that will go to any lengths to obtain planning permission in areas they consider suitable. Even where such applications are initially refused, often the developer wins on appeal; they can afford a highly experienced and expensive barrister that both the council and local NIMBYs (not in my backyarders) have no chance of defending.

This very scenario happened in our village of Henfield not long before we moved away. 10 years ago a friend purchased a lovely detached house with a decent but not huge rear garden backing onto open fields. No doubt you have already guessed that by hook or by crook, a developer obtained planning to construct not one, but over 100 houses on this field. When our friends purchased, at the time it seemed there was absolutely no prospect of development. Times however move on, and pressures on the local authorities increase. Something had to give and in this instance the field in question was the most logical spot for the next development.

Sadly, our friends now look out on to a brick wall. You can get compensation for certain changes that effect your house, like the impact of street lights, road alterations that increase noise etc. Sadly there is no compensation for the loss of a view. If there was, places like the Shard in London would probably not get built, some might say a good thing, but that's another (multi) stor(e)y.

Not all is lost however. There are steps you can take to mitigate this risk, I know of at least one specialist search company that looks not only at current planning applications, but also the potential for future development that could affect an area. The company owner was once a developer himself, so let's face it, he should know. This is worth every penny, especially if you are buying for a view or peace and quiet.

In the meantime you can do your own research simply by looking at the way an area has grown and where it might seem logical for a developer to target.

On a smaller scale consider asking the neighbours whether they have any plans to develop or extend their property. Provided they cooperate, you will be informed of potential inconvenience in the future and hopefully one that is only a short term inconvenience.

Environmental Factors

There are invisible environmental factors that potentially impact the location of your potential new home, for example radon gas. These are usually flagged up in an environmental search which is arranged by solicitors, but there are also other factors you can watch for, some obvious, some less so.

The potential impact of electro-magnetic waves are a genuine concern but any potential adverse effects are as yet unproven. It is not surprising therefore that pylons, mobile phone masts and electricity substations can worry some potential buyers. Pylons and masts should be obvious but a buyer will not always notice them while focused purely on the house. So do look beyond the boundaries and check the land in the immediate vicinity. Electricity substations are often nestled by a garden wall so have a good look around the boundaries.

Some say the cyclical vibration and background rumble of a wind turbine can be unsettling. Others consider them a modern wonder. Turbines are often built on farmland. If you're buying near a farm, have a word with the local farmer in case he has plans or perhaps find out if he has been approached for example by a mobile phone company.

Solar farms are increasingly commonplace; unless you love the limelight, being caught it the reflection could be invasive. A solar farm near Whitland in Carmarthen-shire, south west Wales, has received complaints regarding the impact of glare upon local roads. A house owner could be permanently affected.

For some hazards, you don't need to use your eyes; your nose will tell you more. Sewage treatment works, pig and poultry farms can create quite nauseous odours. If the wind is blowing in the opposite direction when you view a house, you probably will not notice. When you move in, you could be in for an unpleasant surprise. In the UK, the prevailing wind is from the south west, so if the farm is to the north, there is unlikely to be a persistent problem unless it really is on your doorstep. If however it is to the south, prepare for the worst, especially on a hot day.

If you are buying in a rural spot with no mains drains, the house might have a private drainage system. If it is not a modern installation such as a biodigester, and is or example a dated cesspool or septic tank, expect more direct odours, especially in the line of the prevailing winds.

There are countless other considerations. For example you might be buying in close proximity to a stadium. The Olympic Stadium was a joyous venue and during the games, many happy people walked past houses approaching the venue. It is now however, the ground of

West Ham United football club and no doubt the club's supporters have a slightly different vocabulary, especially on a bad day (they have quite a few of those…..).

Inevitably these factors impact your enjoyment of a home, as well as saleability. So even if you are not concerned, others might be and the value of your home could be affected when you come to sell in the future.

Modern or old?

Just like us humans, homes come in all shapes and sizes from the young fit and superefficient, to the sedate energy sapper.

You may have in mind the perfect cottage, Georgian mansion, modern flat etc. But what are the practical implications, advantages and disadvantages of these assorted styles? A survey will of course tell you exactly what you are taking on once you have made your offer and are in a position to purchase (you will find more about surveys in Chapter 8). However, before you start throwing a few offers around, here are a few things to contemplate that you may not have considered and might well change your view of the perfect home.

The Shiny New Home

Buying a spanking brand-new property has several advantages. The most significant is the high levels of insulation and the likelihood of very small energy bills.

As a rule, new properties have limited character and therefore when you resell, anyone looking for period or character property will not be interested. Of course the converse can apply; some people are very attracted by ultra-contemporary design. Nevertheless, these styles can become unfashionable very quickly. Take the current fad for installing bifold doors. These are now so popular that even mainstream developers are installing them but let's be honest, how often in this country do we get the chance to open them fully? Unless it is an exceptional summer, probably just a few days a year. The rest of the time, the vertical lines impact your view. It is not surprising, therefore, that many leading architects are already dropping them in favour of larger single panel windows and sliding doors, rather like the good old patio doors (although they would not dream of calling them that).

Like a brand-new car, a new house is more expensive than second hand. This is understandable, you won't have to carry out any major work for a few years. It is, however, second-hand the moment you plant your bottom on the sofa. Just as the moment you drive your new car out of the showroom, you leave several thousand pounds outside the front door the moment you sign on the dotted line. If you think you may need to sell quickly, buying new is not a good idea, especially if you are competing with other new developments in the area.

New houses are not without their structural problems. The build guarantees do give some reassurance but do not always pay out when you might expect them to. For example, a house full of wonderful glazing is a beautiful thing but if they go wrong, they are not usually covered in the new build guarantee and can be incredibly expensive to replace. Often there is a window manufacturers guarantee, but sometimes the guarantors can disappear leaving you with a very nasty bill (a good reason to get a survey, even if the property is new).

If, like me, you have the DIY skills of 6 month old Great Dane, this is perhaps another good reason to buy new, but do not expect to escape completely. Unless you have absolutely no personal belongings and love waking up in the summer at 4 o'clock in the morning, somebody has got to put up those shelves and window blinds.

If you are a first-time buyer, you are quite likely one of the millennials not entirely sure what the expression DIY means let alone have any proficiency in building trades. This certainly applies to my children. One of them recently rifled through the contents of my toolbox and found it extraordinary that I should be the owner of such exotic equipment, like pliers and an adjustable spanner.

Like many of my age, I helped my parents decorate our house from top to bottom, albeit extremely distastefully and to a poor standard. Today we are used to paying somebody else to 'do it'. I refer to my earlier comments on laziness. If you do not know one end of an electric screw driver from the other, it is probably best to get someone else to hang the shelves. Otherwise be prepared for some clattering noises in the middle of the night; I am referring to the bracket 'securing' your television to the wall, not your partner falling down the stairs because they still think they are in the ground floor flat you were renting the week before.

Period property

The other end of the scale is the lovely period home. The main advantage of a classic period dwelling, provided it has been looked after properly, is the wonderful character. When selling such properties, estate agents suddenly become extraordinarily flowery in their prose, with the use of words that frankly should be banned, such as 'characterful'. Chocolate box, unique, and 'a wealth of timbers' are commonplace.

Period property has an increasing rarity factor. No one yet has discovered a way of building a new period house. There are of course attempts but rarely are these successful and often appear exactly what they are; artificial. Possessing a period property means you own a proportionally diminishing product. Add that to a quality location and you really are on a sound foundation (although it has to be said, many period buildings have no foundation at all).

The disadvantage, of course is that it won't be in tiptop condition even if refurbished. There will always be things to do, for example patching windows, addressing a bit of damp etc. When you move in, you will probably discover various quirks. In our last house we had a whistling chimneybreast. Only in high winds, at other times that would have been…unsettling.

Many period properties are listed, adding further complications, especially if you want to make changes.

This is an important subject, so there is more on the implications of owning a listed building later in this chapter.

As a rule of thumb, the older the property, the greater the potential maintenance liability. The wonderful 'chocolate box' houses referred to by our eloquent estate agents have the thinnest of walls and probably a few rotten timbers embedded in the structure, and that tapping at night is not a ghostly child knocking on your window, but probably the sound of deathwatch beetle enjoying a midnight feast.

Personally, the Edwardian era is my favourite. Although I love Georgian housing, as a surveyor I understand the surprises that can be found when you delve into the structure. For me, Victorians were not particularly creative and could be over elaborate. The Edwardians tended to keep it simple but also learnt from the mistakes of previous generations without the cost cutting and rushed construction that became common pace later in the 20th century, especially in the 1970s. A nice chunky Edwardian house with big windows is a wonderful thing.

A well maintained period property will always hold its value in comparison to others in the locality, but do however expect a few draughts and higher energy bills.

A house or flat?

If you can afford to buy a house, don't discount entirely the option of a flat, there can be considerable advantages. A well-managed block takes most of the maintenance worry away and is handy if you are a busy person with little time to arrange repairs, let alone attempt that dreaded DIY. A secure block is also a good bet if you are likely to be away a lot.

On the other hand, if the building is not well-managed you could be in for some nasty surprises. This is where a good surveyor and solicitor working together really come into their own. The surveyor will look at the building to see how well it is maintained, and the solicitor will ask for management records to see how much there is in the pot for spending on unexpected repairs, planned maintenance and generally if there is a good management record. A badly managed building will deteriorate and the flat owners can end up with a shocking bill. In the case of complex period buildings with just a few flats, the cost to each individual flat owner can be catastrophic.

A case in point is a rather lovely building near East Grinstead that was converted into some amazing apartments back in the mid-20th-century. The setting is quite magical. A friend purchased one of the flats some years after it was converted. At the time, management was adequate and it was known that some repairs would be required in the future. The leaseholders however made the mistake of managing repair and maintenance themselves, instead of employing a professional organisation such as a firm of chartered building surveyors, or at least an experienced management company.

Consequently, external redecoration was piecemeal and important repairs such as leaking gutters, defects in the roof and so on were delayed. In the end, the owners could delay matters no further and called in a firm of professionals who carried out a detailed inspection of the entire fabric. The cost of the remedial measures required was so significant, that at least two of the 15 flat owners had to sell up as they had no means of raising their share of the repair bill. For my friend, this was a particular heartache as she had lived there for years but had little resource to meet the cost. If they had only paid a little bit more each year into the maintenance fund, and carried out that little bit of extra work, they would not now be in this calamitous position and needless to say, the value of the flats would be considerably more.

Another disadvantage of the older conversions is poor sound insulation. Until the late 20th century, there was virtually no requirement in this respect, and is not uncommon to hear your neighbours walking around let alone having a party.

Modern conversions and flats are a better option in this respect as stringent sound insulation standards must be met. Newbuild flats are however, not without their problems. I have seen many cases where the flats have been finished with supposedly maintenance free products such as specialist external renders, timber cladding, metal windows etc., only for these finishes to deteriorate after just a few years. Whilst the cost of redecorating in the first 10 or 15 years was saved, the higher cost of having to repair the specialist finishes far outweighed the initial savings.

Boring but important…. freehold or leasehold

Most flats have a leasehold tenure. You solicitor will explain the full implications, but basically this means that you do not own the property one hundred percent. Instead, flat owners will hold a long lease for say 99 years and there is usually an entirely separate freehold. The leaseholders pay a small annual charge to the freeholder, known as the ground rent.

As time goes by, the lease shortens and the value of your property reduces. If you do not renew the lease, eventually the flat simply returns to the freeholder. You do however have a legal right to extend the lease if you want. It is sensible to extend it before the remaining lease period falls below 80 years. After that it becomes increasingly expensive to extend the lease and it can be impossible to get a mortgage from a mainstream lender.

Freeholds are usually owned by investors. Often a freeholder will sell his interest to a third party. The value of the freehold will depend on several factors including the length of the leases, and the ground rent charge. The ground rent used to be a small annual fee paid the freeholder, often known as a 'peppercorn rent', i.e. just a pound. Over the years when renewing leases, freeholders have changed the goalposts and now it is not uncommon for the ground rent to be around £100 a year, and stepped up during the term of the lease. So it might be that you buy a flat with a relatively cheap ground rent and then find after five years the annual charge is raised. By the end of the lease, the figure can be quite considerable.

Cheeky developers.

Take.you.to.the.cleaners
Development Company Limited

Recently some developers have not only developed their buildings, but also developed an underhand source of additional revenue. By creating leases with ground rent charges that increase periodically, they are able to sell the freehold for considerable sums. In fact, they have even taken to building estates of houses with leasehold interest, using the excuse that there are communal grounds and paths to be maintained by a common freeholder. The investor will hang onto it for a bit and sell for a profit or enjoys the healthy and usually high increasing ground rent charges, and the home owners face much higher charges to extend their leases. This is not as yet common practice and your solicitor will most likely point out the potential long term costs, but do ensure you are fully informed as the value of the home could diminish quicker than you anticipate.

The government is currently producing legislation to overcome this abuse of the leasehold tenure, which in my view is nothing less than another property fraud, but for some purchasers it is too late. Eventually the practice will be stopped, but there will remain rogue leases created prior to the proposed legislation so be careful you do not end up with one of those.

Buying the freehold.

Leaseholders have a legal right to buy the freehold provided there are enough owners interested. This is useful if you want to take control of the building management. The freeholder controls maintenance and charges the leaseholders not just for the work, but also for the trouble. Ultimately as a leaseholder you have to pay for repair and maintenance but it should be a fair charge and the work should be carried out diligently. Sometimes you can take legal action to buy the freehold if it can be proved the existing freeholder is not carrying out his duty under the terms of the lease, usually relating to repair and maintenance.

You should still hand the management over to a professional though. You don't want to end up in the same mess as our friends in East Grinstead.

Houses.

A house is usually a freehold interest so you do not have all the common problems associated with leasehold flats, shared maintenance etc. and therefore you do not have a maintenance charge to pay. There are exceptions, sometimes there are other common facilities such as roads, share gardens etc. to maintain.

Usually however, if you own the house freehold, i.e. outright, you have no nasty maintenance charge to pay. You do however have to get those windows painted, repair the gutters and so on and it is very easy to ignore these essential works when you are busy doing something far more interesting. So although there is no maintenance charge to pay, there is still a cost and inconvenience of arranging upkeep, something that many people do not consider when buying on a budget. If you buy a house and do not maintain it properly, it will lose value.

Listed buildings.

Whether you are buying a house or flat, during your search for a home you are likely at some stage to encounter a building that is listed. These buildings are quite literally on a list held and controlled by Historic England and are best described as the Local Conservation Officer's favourite pets.

There are three categories of listing. The least stringent but still awkward is Grade II. More stringent and frankly inconvenient is Grade II*, and then there is Grade I, where you are required to talk in Old English and dress in a style that matches the period of the house, handy if you are a fan of 1980s new romantic and own a Georgian house.

I am being facetious of course, and in fact my practice is a member of SPAB, the Society for the Protection of Ancient Buildings.

If you are the owner of a listed building, you are not just living in a building of historic importance, you are a custodian for future generations. The protection of our most important buildings and other structures is essential to protect our built heritage.

There is a common misconception that only the exterior of the building is listed. In fact the interior is often more precious than the exterior. The entire building including the interior layout and fittings such as the fireplaces, doors, skirting boards, cornices etc. and the outside up to the main perimeter garden boundaries cannot be altered without listed building consent.

Making unauthorised changes is a criminal offence and the owners are responsible for all unauthorised works *including* those carried out by past owners. This only applies to changes that have been made since the building was listed. Most were listed in the early 1950s. At the time, the planning officers simply drove around and described the exterior of the building from what they could see from the nearest public area. Often the descriptions were vague and inaccurate. The first the owners would know about it would be a letter in the post telling them they were unable to sneeze in their own home without first obtaining permission from English Heritage, the organisation responsible for the list before Historic England was created.

Often, therefore, the authority will have very limited records about the interior or parts that cannot be seen from the road unless there have been subsequent applications for alterations and the conservation officer has visited the property.

Planners often consider past changes an integral part of the building history, even that 1960's carbuncle stuck on the side. You cannot, therefore, assume they will allow removal of apparently poorly designed features. If you own a listed building, it is essential you inform the conservation officer of any planned changes you are making, even if these are seemingly simple repairs, for example, that potentially will damage lath and plaster ceilings or wattle and daub finishes.

Obviously this poses quite a problem if you are buying a house that needs refurbishment and you would like to change the interior or extend the footprint. These alterations might be critical to your decision to buy a house but you cannot guarantee approval will be given until the application has been made, creating quite a dilemma if you are really keen on the house.

So it is essential you find out early on in the process, ideally before you make an offer, whether the house is listed and what the implications are to your plans.

Do not assume a period property is, or is not listed. It is not just the style of the building that counts, an important aspect of the building's history is often a factor. Examples of unusual listed buildings include the only example in England of American style canopies at an Esso petrol station in Red Hill, Leicestershire, and a large bus station in Preston, built in 1969, considered by many to be an eyesore.

In fact, it doesn't even have to be a building; even the zebra crossing on the cover of the Beatles album, Abbey Road, is listed.

The agent's particulars will usually indicate if a property is listed, but often the information is omitted. In fact on more than one occasion I have inspected property described by the agent *and the owner* as listed but in fact it was not. Needless to say my client was rather pleased as the house needed work and numerous potential hurdles were suddenly removed by this revelation.

So before you start wasting your money on solicitors fees and envisaging that fantastic glass box extension, search the Historic England list online at

https://www.historicengland.org.uk/listing/the-list/

Be sure you check thoroughly as some addresses are inaccurate; the previous owners, Carolyn and Kevin, might have changed Wisteria Cottage to Kevolyn Towers, (this is a fun game, my wife Claire and I could own Clob Cottage....), so if in doubt, call the local planners.

If the house is listed, your conveyancer and surveyor can then explain the implications. As surveyors, it is our responsibility not only to check the condition of a building, but also advise of any potential non-conformant changes made which might have to be addressed.

Chapter Summary

- Location is one of, if not the, biggest factors in choosing a home.

- If a house seems a bargain, there is usually a good reason.

- Don't just view the house, check out the immediate neighbouring area at both day and night times.

- If necessary, ask specialists to assess the likelihood of nearby development.

- Are you a modern or period home person? Consider the implications of both.

- New houses are like new homes; as soon as you buy them they are second hand and can lose value.

- If buying a flat, make sure the management company is well run and there are sufficient maintenance funds for emergency works and planned maintenance.

- Avoid leasehold tenure with unreasonably escalating ground rents.

- If you are buying a listed building, make sure your conveyancer and surveyor explain the full implications.

CHAPTER 5

Buying *and* Selling - Advice for the Seller

If you have nothing to sell, I suggest you skip the next section (for now that is, if you are a first-time buyer, hopefully you WILL have a home to sell soon if you wish).

Those that are lucky enough to own a home but have not moved for a while and need advice, read on.

If you are serious about moving, you simply *must* get your home on the market and under offer. Don't look if you haven't sold! A first time buyer is in a great position to make an offer. If, however, you already own and are moving up or down the property ladder, you really should not be looking too seriously yet; you simply must be under offer' and in a completed chain.

The agents are obliged to inform the vendors of all offers, regardless of the prospective purchasers position, but will recommend to the owners that the house you love should remain on the market until you are in a position to proceed. In fact, until you are in such a position, it really is best not to look as your hopes might be dashed. Your position to proceed is key to a successful negotiation.

If you want to swoop quickly, it might even be worthwhile completing your sale and taking rented accommodation. Collapsing chains are commonplace and the risk of falling at the final hurdle can be nerve jangling. The longer the chain, the more likelihood of collapse.

Going in to rented is however also a quite risky option; you must be certain you want out. It might take far longer to find your dream home then you expected; prices could rise and you no doubt will not be entirely happy in temporary accommodation. Packing boxes once, let alone twice is not fun and you will invariably put the wrong items into storage. Just make sure the bottle opener is to hand.

Selling your Home

In recent years, even the simplest of decisions in life have become increasingly complex purely by the sheer number of options available. Last time I checked, there were 38 styles of coffee. By the time you have made your choice, your morning break is nearly over.

Thankfully, when it comes to selling a home, while the options have increased, the choices remain relatively simple.

- The traditional estate agent.

Most people still opt for a local estate agent to sell their home.

There is a very good reason for this. The estate agent acts as a buffer between you and people viewing your house. You can go out while they show people around. You don't have to listen to the negative comments about your three porcelain ducks on the wall, or the positive behaviour from people that don't want to offend by displaying a lack of interest and in the meantime raise false hopes.

Eventually someone will make an offer. After that, the agent will deal with them directly and earn their keep by tracking the sale and doing the upmost holding things together.

Most agents charge around 1.5% of the final transaction fee, so if your house is on the market for £160,000, and you accept an offer of £150,000 which then continues to completion, the fee at a rate of 1.5% would be £2,250. Don't forget the VAT, currently set at 20% which adds another £450, so the total fee would be £2,700.

Usually you should use just one agent, known as the sole agent. If you go to several, known as multi agent marketing, you will pay a higher fee and it also smacks of desperation so best to avoid this unless there is a very good reason; for example, if your house is in a rural position, you might want to try to two independents in separate nearby towns.

The fee is usually paid on completion by the solicitor directly to the agent, so you can't disappear to the Cayman Islands without paying.

Choosing an Agent

Estate agents fees might seem high, and yes, those operating at the top end of the market can survive on just a few sales per year. It easy to forget, however, that they do not get paid if sales fall through, and furthermore the fee is always the same regardless of how long the process takes. Our poor estate agent in Henfield village had to wait six months before getting their fee and in the interim dealt with five sales that fell through. Obviously, a painful process for everyone concerned, especially my wife and I, but we got there in the end and frankly, the agents fee was worth every penny.

Of course, there are some agents who are not diligent and frankly give a poor service. When choosing the agent don't just look at the fees they charge, check their sales progression techniques. If they are not tracking and chasing the chain, avoid. There is nothing worse than the estate agent that doesn't keep you informed. Again, I've made this mistake before. A letting agent in Brighton that managed a flat for me offered to sell it. It turned out they were great at letting but pretty useless at selling. It took two weeks before I was told a purchaser had disappeared off the radar!

I changed agents and sold immediately.

Here is a check list for choosing an agent:

Are they part of a professional organisation such as the NAEA (http://www.naea.co.uk/).

What online portals do they use?

What is the quality of the particulars prepared for other homes, both in print and online?

Are there enough pictures and are they both representative and an appropriate quality that show your home it its best light? I have seen particulars with pants on the washing line.

Will they produce floor plans, in my opinion, essential, but not always provided, especially if the fee is 'competitive'.

What other advertising techniques will they use?

Will your home be in the shop window?

What days and hours of the week are they open?

How many properties do they have under offer compared to overall availability (a high sales proportion suggest sensible valuing and good sales chasing).

Have they sold others in your street or neighbourhood recently?

Will they vet and accompany all prospects (viewing by nosey people is not uncommon if the agent has not checked properly).

How do they arrive at the valuation? Over optimism will get you excited and persuaded to use them, but ultimately disappointed when, 6 weeks down the line, they suggest a reduction in the asking price.

Are they part of a large corporate or local independent? The latter may well know the local market better and will not be hassling prospective vendors with secondary sources of income by offering to arrange mortgages etc.

Sometimes the corporate will favour a buyer who is obtaining a mortgage through their financial services arm, but this might not be the best buyer for you. Also, now all agents lodge details online, the corporates no longer have the advantage of a wider reach.

- Online agents.

For many years there has been talk of online agents disrupting the residential sales market. Up until now, most attempts at doing so have proved largely unsuccessful.

Recently there is a more disrupting effect with new companies appearing almost monthly and making a decent fist of it. In fact it is predicted that the current leaders in the market, Purple Bricks, could control as much as 10% of the market in the next few years, a frightening prospect for the traditional agent.

Online estate agents tend to charge a flat fee of between £300 and £1,500, regardless of the value of your property, so are considerably cheaper. The fee structure varies, some are very cheap with set fees to register and advertise your property, others have a part set fee and commission arrangement.

They will help with valuation advice and load the information onto their website and the online portals.

So a no brainer, yes? Well, you get what you pay for. In return for the cheap fees, you often have to arrange viewings directly with potential buyers and in the event of a sale, carry out the sales chasing yourself. This is hard enough for the agents, but if you own the house, have lived in it and loved it, be prepared for a protracted and painful process.

Understandably, traditional estate agents have a severe dislike for online agents; a familiar pattern throughout the disrupting online industry (next time you are in a Black Cab, if you want to arrive at you destination without an ear-bashing, don't mention Uber).

It is not just because the low fees that irk them, but also because they find it difficult to hold chains together if they have to deal directly with vendors who have no experience in the market, instead of a representing agent. I know of at least one agent in Brighton who refuses to deal with any prospective purchaser if their property has sold or is selling through an online agent. Many others certainly avoid them. If you have sold through one and the market is busy, don't be surprised if you keep missing out on your next purchase.

While there certainly seems to be a surge in online agent presence, their future success remains uncertain. Some seem to make the money purely out of the registration process and often individuals end up turning to a conventional agent when the online company proves unsuccessful, so end up paying twice. There again,

I know someone who sold within a week through an online agent and the whole procedure was very smooth.

There are also now some very effective hybrids entering the market, and the disruption process clearly is far from over. I know of one rapidly growing practice that operates only t the high end, and provide a very personal service.

Preparing for Sale

So, you have made a sudden decision to sell your home. The agent has only just left but has already arranged the EPC and called to say he has a person in mind that might be interested. The first viewing is on the horizon! You wander into your teenage son's bedroom, a mysterious cave in the corner of the house where you rarely venture, and realise the black painted walls plastered with posters of Slipknot are, well, not ideal.

Worry not, most people understand your house is not an art gallery with fine lines and minimal furniture; it is lived in and will be shown in the light for which it is used. On the other hand, most buyers are not interior designers and will struggle to visualise your house with their stuff in. It is important to do what you can to show your home in a favourable light in the limited time you have available between deciding to sell and that first viewing.

You would be surprised how just a few small changes requiring just a little time and virtually no money, can significantly increase the chances of selling your home, and in some circumstances, can even increase the value.

Here is a list of catastrophic mistakes to avoid and simple changes that can make your house far more desirable and help you to achieve the highest price in the quickest possible time.

1. First Impressions

The last thing you want is a purchaser to approach your house and then drive off without even getting out of the car. First impressions are more important than anything else you can do to improve saleability. You might not necessarily be a gardener, but we are all capable of cutting the lawn, trimming the hedge and sweeping the path and drive. Keeping the front garden tidy will make a huge difference to the initial impression you give. And of course a mattress in the garden? NO!

2. A lick of Paint

Tatty decorations can give a false impression that there is a whole lot of work to do. For the non DIY buyer this can be a real turn off. Some buyers might be wary and think other things could be wrong.

If you have some time to spare before the home is on the market, with a couple of pots and paint and some elbow grease, you can transform a tired looking house to an appealing home.

If you haven't got the time, it's worth paying somebody to do this for you, the chances are you'll get more than your money back with a good offer. Keep the colours neutral. You might think the Zebra stripes in the hall are cool but everyone's taste is different. The teenagers room might have to stay black though. Believe me, the only thing that is more important than house presentation is avoiding the wrath of a young adult.

3. Don't Buy a Cheap Front Door

You can buy plastic double glazed doors extremely cheaply but unfortunately that is exactly how they look, cheap. If you already have a wooden front door it is cheaper to renovate and paint it and it looks so much better. In fact, a new wooden door is often cheaper than plastic one where the cost includes the salesman's hefty commission.

4. Tidy the house

It may sound bizarre, but you'd be surprised how many people do not tidy up properly before a viewing. Cleaning the kitchen, putting things away and making the beds will make all the difference to the presentation of the house. Flowers on the table are a lovely touch. The smell of fresh coffee and bread in the oven is however probably a step too far; you are not a café.

5. Hide the Clutter

Most people have lots of personal bits and pieces on display that are extremely meaningful for them, for example numerous photographs, holiday trinkets, ornaments etc. These mean nothing to a prospective purchaser and while a few pieces are to be expected, there is a fine line between homely and a second-hand shop. Ideally you should remove the majority of them when the house is being viewed; you can always put them back afterwards. This may make the house seem bare to you but remember; the simpler the presentation, the easier it is for a buyer to visualise the home as their own.

6. Keep the House a Comfortable Temperature

It goes without saying that a freezing cold house is unwelcoming, and a hot one has a similar impact. If it is a cold day outside, viewers will probably have their coats on and the last thing they want is to get boiling hot while viewing your house; it will only encourage an early exit.

By all means, light the fire if you've got one (not in the summer; that's just wrong...), but make sure a window is open too.

7. Stay Odour Free and Control your Pets

If you have a dog or other pets, the combination of animals and a hot house will soon turn off your potential buyers. The chances are you have become immune to your pet's aromas, but the buyers will notice immediately. They may even mistake the smell for a damp problem. Make sure you open the windows and freshen up the house a good hour or so before the buyers arrive (don't overdo the air freshener). If your dog is jumpy and barks at people coming to the door, arrange for someone to take him out.

I remember an occasion, when viewing a house for myself, being hit by the smell of a wet dog which then proceeded to follow me round from room to room. The owners' thought it was amusing and don't get me wrong, I am a dog lover, but I was there to view the house and found the puppy quite a distraction. I left remembering the dog and not the house.

8. Don't Follow Buyers Around

Viewers hate the vendor following them around. Usually the agents' details will have a floor plan so unless you have a hidden passage, they can see exactly where everything is. Let them wander and get a feel for the house. Detailed information is no use to them at this stage when all they are thinking about is the big picture; i.e. could they live here? They don't need to be told that you've just had the boiler serviced and there is an extra socket by the television; that isn't going to make them buy the property. Leave them to it so they can get a feel for the place. If you don't like the idea of leaving them wandering on their own, go out and ask the agent to accompany. Also, the agent is more likely to get honest feedback.

9. Don't Offer the Viewer a Drink as Soon as they Arrive

When the buyer arrives all they are thinking of is your home and what it looks like. If you offer them a drink they will either have to say no, or they will end up having to carry it around. Also if they are really not interested, they might end up feeling they have to stay and be polite when all they want to do is leave. If their visit is prolonged, that's a good sign, but offering a drink should be avoided until there is an offer on the table.

10. And Finally........

If you are still getting little interest it can really only mean one thing; you're asking too much money. As much as we all like to think our house is the best in the neighbourhood, ultimately the market dictates the value. Everything is sellable at the right price. If reducing the asking price is an option for you, take action quickly, say after first two or three months at most. If you do not reduce reasonably quickly, the house could soon become part of what many agents describe as 'old stock'. The agents lose enthusiasm for your property and many potential buyers will have already discounted it, even if you do eventually reduce the price some months down the line. In the meantime, you could be missing opportunities to buy your dream home.

Other Options

1. Sit Tight and Wait.

You can simply wait in the hope someone will eventually make an offer. Very occasionally, the right buyer eventually appears even if the price is a little high. If your house is similar to others in the area, you will have to wait for most of them to sell therefore reducing the buyer's options. In a falling market, however, this is dangerous, you will simply chase the market down and eventually sell for far less than if you asked a sensible price in the first place. In a rising market, the house of your dreams will become increasingly less affordable while you wait for a buyer.

2. Auction your home

This is not such a daft idea. People think there is a catch when they see a property at auction but usually it is simply that the vendor wants to move quickly.

There will be a reserve price below which the house cannot be sold, so do not worry that someone might be buying your home for a song. The auctioneer however will not be interested unless the reserve price is sensible. If you are lucky, over excited bidders might even pay more than you hoped. This would, however, be quite unusual.

3. When all else fails, take a massive risk and get a bridging loan.

If you need to act quickly, the answer might be a bridging loan. Provided you can raise a reasonable deposit, some specialist banks will lend you the money to buy a property while you look for a buyer of your existing home, so problem solved yes? Well not exactly. The arrangement fees and interest rates are high and of course there is the risk you either do not sell for as much as you hoped, or it takes longer than expected and you could end up seriously out of pocket.

The banks will only lend if they are comfortable with the risk. They take the advice of a professional valuer; so too should you. You may disagree with the valuers opinion; but remember, they are assessing the property without any emotional attachment, and are probably right.

The significant difference is the bank can afford the hit if it all goes horribly wrong, but the chances are, you cannot. A bridging loan should be taken only if you are certain you can afford the hefty charges and potential losses. In my experience, this option is feasible only if the property you are buying is an absolute steal, which is rarely the case, or is a development opportunity.

Really Unusual Property

There is sometimes another reason a home sticks on the market; you really do have an unusual and unique residence. If so, it is simply a question of patience; eventually a buyer will appear and when they do come along, will almost certainly fall in love with the property and pay anything that is required to get their hands on it. Just as you have been waiting an age for the perfect buyer, they may have been waiting for just the right home.

We once owned a four bedroom house with virtually no garden but a with superb view; great for someone that loves open spaces but hates gardening. Not necessarily especially unique, but no good for your average family with a budding David Beckham. The right buyer did however appear, and with a very reasonable offer. We just had to be patient.

In another instance, my practice once surveyed an estate with three 'period' thatched cottages that were actually less than 15 years old. A purpose-built ruin (seriously) was constructed on the land and there was not just one, but three sets of security gates. Needless to say, the buyer, an American A list celebrity that will remain nameless, thought they were buying a cute piece of English heritage. Now that was the ultimate unique home and buyer combi; hats off to the buying agent.

Do not, however, think that your home is unique when clearly it is not; that gorgeous dog parlour is actually a utility room to most buyers and does not justify adding £20,000 to the asking price.

Chapter Summary

- Do not start looking for a home until your house is under offer.

- If you sell and move to temporary accommodation puts you in a very strong buying position, but can be twice the stress.

- When choosing an estate agent, choose quality above fee; the chances are you will sell for more, and the service will be better.

- A few simple changes to your home can make a huge difference to saleability and even value.

- If you are struggling to sell, almost without fail, the reason is because the asking price is too high.

- Unusual property can take longer to sell.

- Other options such as auctioning your home and taking bridging loans are possible options but hold risks.

CHAPTER 6

Start Looking!

Okay, so you've established your budget, checked out the area, understand the implications of listed buildings, decided your preference for old, modern, flat or house, and know how to spot a noisy neighbour.

If you are a first-time buyer, or an owner with home that is under offer, now is the time to start looking in earnest.

How to find the house of your dreams

The dawn of the internet has made it so much easier to search for property. Gone are the days of trawling around the agents in each town, missing a few on the way. Every estate agent enters the details into one of the four main online portals; Rightmove, Zoopla, Prime Location and Onthemarket.

You will find some properties are advertised on just one or two of these sites so you need to look at them all. The portals are similar but have quite useful individual quirks. For example, Prime Location gives the option to filter the listings in order of most reduced asking price. This gives you an idea of how much property prices might be falling in a certain area. Beware however, this is misleading if the original asking price was unrealistically high in the first place. You will also see how long homes have been listed. The longer they have been on, the greater potential for negotiation.

There is a snag with relying purely on the portals. Properties normally appear online a few days after they have been taken on. For a start, a property cannot be advertised officially until the Energy Performance Certificate (the EPC) has been completed. By the time the agent has produced the particulars and the vendor has verified the accuracy of the description, usually several days have passed. If you are looking in an area of high demand, you might find your ideal home has been sold before it is even listed online. So if you have the time, do still take the time to register personally with the agents.

If you are a first time buyer, cash buyer or have a house in a completed chain, in other words, the start of the chain is complete, the agents will prioritise you over others that are simply browsing the market or not yet in a position to proceed. A good agent will call you as soon as they take on something they consider of interest. They will of course also phone up with property that is seemingly entirely unsuited. Don't get too irritated by this; they are salesmen and that is what they are trained to do. In fact, you might well end up buying something you didn't think you wanted at a price you thought you could not afford in an area you thought you did not like. So, don't discount entirely what they suggest, even estate agents are right sometimes (sorry agents, I'm trying to stick up for you).

Sometimes, however, it seems there is absolutely nothing of interest to you, no matter how hard you look. This could be the time to turn to a specialist buyer that can search on your behalf.

Bring on The Buying agent.

If you've not been involved in the property market for the last 20 years you almost certainly will have missed the rise of the buying agent. A buying agent is like an estate agent in reverse. You pay an estate agent to sell your property, a buying agent is paid to find you one.

In some countries, for example, Dubai, employing a buying agent is normal practice, especially for expats unfamiliar with local practice.

In America, agents act for each party, so there is a buying and a selling agent. Both earn around 3%, so a total of 6% of the value goes to the agent on completion of the deal.

Most buying agents will operate only in the pricier sector of the market, usually £1,000,000 plus. There are however, a few, especially outside London, that will take on purchases at a lower level. Using a buying agent might be viewed as an extravagance but if you do have the ability to pay their commission and monthly retainer you will be one step ahead of the market.

A strong buying agent has numerous connections and know their patch backwards. They are often socialites and anything they don't know about the local property market and the main movers and shakers is not worth knowing.

A good buying agent can prove particularly useful if you are not local. They will sift through and view properties on your behalf, and discuss the options with you. In fact the chances are they will have seen many of the properties in the patch before you have even instructed them, discounting those that are clearly unsuitable therefore saving you an enormous amount of time.

They will also carry out all negotiations on your behalf making it far easier to hold your nerve at the 'squeaky bum' stage, as Alex Ferguson would say.

We receive numerous instructions from buying agents and often the property has not reached the general market. Just recently, we surveyed a property that the buying agent had found by contacting the owners directly. This was not a cold call, the owners were previous clients of the buying agent and had indicated they would be moving again within a few years. As the building suited the new buyers' criteria, everyone was a winner and before you could say the words 'estate agents commission', the vendors sold and the buyer found the house of their dreams before anyone else had the chance to pull the rug from under their feet.

Such transactions are known as 'off market' and are surprisingly common place at the top end of the market, a mysterious layer that most people do not even know exists. In fact, a high-end agent national agent claimed recently that as many as 20% of their sales are off market.

For the average first-time buyer, the use of a buying agent is probably a step too far. For others though, their services can prove invaluable. After an initial consultation where they will gain a full understanding of your requirements, they will set about the market in your chosen geographical area using their underground network of local contacts.

If you are prepared to put your hand in your pocket, a buying agent will increase your chances of finding your ideal home and is perhaps not such an extravagance after all.

Choosing a buying agent

If you are lucky (or perhaps savvy) enough to afford a buying agent, here are a few questions you should ask them before signing on the dotted line.

1. What is their geographical area? If it is expansive their local knowledge might be limited, However, if they focus on a niche sector, such as farms, they might well know every potential property in the country.

2. Who do they know? Most buying agents cut their teeth with high end estate agents, the likes of Savills, Strutt and Parker and Knight Frank. They keep in touch with their old colleagues and often are informed of properties that are about to enter the market. They have a foot in the door before the rest of the general public. Some would argue this is a restraint of trade and conflict of interest, but until the matter is regulated, it is something the market will have to live with.

3. Find out what deals they have done. They may be restricted by confidentiality, but there is no harm in asking. The best buying agents have several deals under their belt.

4. Ask local estate agents if they are familiar with the buying agent. If they have heard of them, the buying agent is clearly proactive. If the estate agent is effusive, the buying agent is well connected.

Chapter Summary

- If you want to be one of the first people to view a house, register with as many agents as possible, as properties do not appear on the internet portals the first day they are available.
- Many houses sell 'off market'.
- For those with a higher budget, consider using a buying agent.

CHAPTER 7

Making an Offer and Negotiating

Ok, you have found the home of your dreams and all the boxes are ticked. It is time to take a leap of faith and make an offer!

Timing

Rule one: get your offer in now! If you are keen but have some reservations, don't ponder – offer. At worst, you can withdraw. Do not, however, offer and withdraw willy-nilly, you will gain a reputation as a serial time-waster and soon be found out by the agents.

Pitching the offer

If a property has only just come on the market it is pointless making a silly offer, you will be told to go away. Estate agents are obliged to pass on all offers so there is a risk of potentially offending the seller. It is, however, worth chancing your arm if the house has been hanging around. In fact it is likely the owners are under pressure to reduce the price anyway. At worst they will say no and you can increase your offer or walk away.

If the vendor is not in any hurry, often they will simply withdraw from the market until for example the following spring in the hope of improved conditions and a fresh set of potential punters arise. Almost without exception, however, if a property does not sell within a couple of months it is for one of three reasons; the asking price is too high, usually due to an over valuation by the estate agent, the seller is not very serious about moving, or the property is so unusual that the ideal buyer is similarly unique.

Pointless negotiation stand-offs.

The English property market has limited supply; bargains are incredibly rare and unless there is a short term hesitation in the market that has made a few sellers panic (twin towers, the financial crash, Brexit to name a few), invariably you will have to offer close asking price. However, for most people every penny counts and if you hold your nerve you can usually get up to 5% off depending on the circumstances.

On numerous occasions sales fall through simply because there has been a stand-off between the seller and the buyer. A seller might refuse to sell below the magic number of say £300,000 - 'The offer must have a three in front of it!' is a typical position. On the other hand the buyer is refusing to make an offer that does not have a two in front of it. So you can end up with a ridiculous situation where an offer has been made of say £298,00 and the sake of £2000, which frankly in the big picture is minimal, the whole deal collapses.

As a purchaser in these circumstances, you need to focus on the goal and not the detail. If you really want the property that badly, forget about the vendors intransigence and simply make an offer that will be accepted. That £2000 extra will soon be forgotten once you move in and start to enjoy the home. Remember, a house as a home first and investment second. Do not let pride get in the way of your dream move!

Chapter Summary

- If something is suitable, don't hesitate, make an early offer.

- Avoid offensively low offers, especially if the house has not been on the market for long.

- The longer a house has been on the market, the lower you can pitch your first offer.

- Avoid pointless negotiation standoffs

- A house is a home first, and an investment second.

CHAPTER 8

The Lawyer, the Surveyor, and the Candlestick Maker - Bring in the Professionals.

Choosing a lawyer

As soon as your offer is accepted, the first thing the estate agent will ask is 'who is your solicitor?'

Lawyers specialising in buying and selling houses are most commonly known as conveyancers. If you are a first-time buyer, the chances are you've never even heard of a conveyancer or had any cause to contact a solicitor, unless of course, you have found yourself in a sticky situation (ah, those teenage years…).

Choosing your solicitor should not be a complicated exercise but again you are advised to pick someone that specialises.

The one you choose should depend on the type of property you are buying. If you are purchasing a listed building or a property with other complexities, for example, flying freeholds, various rights-of-way etc. you really should try and go to someone experienced in dealing with such complex matters. If you are not a first-time buyer, you may have some experience of dealing with solicitors and have a preferred firm but do still check their credentials in this field.

If, however, you have no preference, it will be very tempting to use the solicitors recommended by the estate agents. The independent agents will tend to recommend independent solicitors, perfectly acceptable provided they have the experience you require. The corporates, however, tend to have agreements with large firms many of which deal purely online and the service provided can be flaky to say the least.

For example an online solicitor can prove very difficult to get hold of not just by you, but other parties in the chain who require information urgently. This is not to say they won't do a good job, it just might take rather a long time, and the longer it takes, the greater chance of things going wrong. Sadly fall throughs in house sales are commonplace, which at best is disappointing, at worst, very distressing.

Obviously the fee is a consideration but on no account should this be your main criteria. This might be an acceptable when buying a kettle, but certainly is not when committing yourself to what is probably one of the most expensive purchase you will ever make.

So here is a list of my criteria when choosing a conveyancer.

- The fee.

  Is this cheap? If so don't expect a good service, delays could arise (the longer it takes, the greater chance of the sale falling through) and mistakes might be made. Avoid.

- Location.

  If you're buying a property that is relatively simple then the conveyancer can frankly be anywhere in the country. You do not have to go to their office to sign paperwork. If however, you are making a complex purchase, a solicitor that is not too far away may know the locality or might even visit the property and walk the grounds to get a feel for potential complications.

- Communication and technology

  Choose a lawyer with good IT communications, and one that will liaise with your surveyor. The surveyor will often be the eyes and ears of the conveyancer and good communication between the two is essential.

- Size of practice

  For the more complex properties, a practice with several divisions might be useful. For example, if there are commercial aspects of the purchase, such as a live work unit, some input from commercial conveyancers could be useful if not essential. If they prove to be good, this might also be an opportunity to build up a longer relationship with the firm for other services.

  The small one-man bands might prove to be exceptionally good value and experienced. There is however, potential delays if they are ill, go on holiday so do ask what their contingency is in such circumstances.

Whoever you choose, make sure they are a member of the Law Society. The law society regulates all firms and ensures they meet certain standards, such as the level of professional indemnity insurance to cover you in case they make a mistake (hopefully not, but errors do occur occasionally).

Next Steps

So you now have your solicitor. The first thing they will do is arrange property 'searches'. Property searches are a crucial step; they reveal vital information that could impact your decision and even your ability to buy the property.

There are several different types of searches your solicitor will conduct when you buy a property.

Local authority searches

These are critical as they will look at all information held by the local authority involving the property, including any prospective plans for nearby new developments or infrastructure projects that could impact you as an owner; the last thing you need is to be told your lovely new home might at some stage be demolished for the town bypass (think 'Hitch Hikers Guide to the Galaxy' when the Vogons destroyed the supercomputer, i.e. earth, with the apparent excuse of building a hyperspace bypass). They will also show who is responsible for maintaining roads and paths adjoining the property.

Land Registry searches

Land registry searches ensure the seller is the legal owner of the property; good to know! Believe it or not there have been several reported cases of fraudsters 'selling' a home they do not own, running away with the money and leaving the poor buyer with nothing but a massive hole in their life savings.

The seller will be named on the title register and title plan at the Land Registry. Check with all parties that the vendor is actually this person.

The land registry should also list any covenants affecting the land.

A covenant is restriction made on a property often imposed by a previous owner. We have two on our home, stating that we cannot extend forward beyond a certain point, and another requiring us to maintain deer fences along certain boundaries. In fact we don't have any deer fences and someone built the garage beyond the front elevation many years ago and no-one seems upset, but there is always a potential risk that we would be asked to take action to meet the covenant criteria.

As a safeguard, you can take out an indemnity insurance. This will not stop the covenant being imposed, but will help cover some of the consequential costs and potential loss in value, if any. That said, many covenants are unenforceable; a solicitor specialising in the subject should be able to tell you if that is the case.

Environmental search

These are seemingly complicated documents but in reality made up of online information that has been documented over the years and produced in a structured format. They will tell you information that can seem quite alarming but in reality often proves insignificant. For example an environmental search may suggest your potential new home is in a high risk area of subsidence. Usually this simply means it is built in an area where there is shrinkable clay where indeed, subsidence does arise more often than on other soil types. However, provided you have had a survey, and the surveyor has not found any movement, you can ignore this information;

an inspection by a surveyor provides the true picture that overrides the online statistical information.

Searches also pin point landfill sites. There are varying types, the most potentially dangerous are those used recently for burying toxic waste including batteries, asbestos etc. Household waste emits methane and can fall into this category.

If your prospective purchase is built on or near one of these, you should withdraw. Certainly it is unlikely you would get a mortgage unless the site has been properly decontaminated, and even if it has, problems could arise on resale.

Other items listed in the search are often innocuous and historic, for example, records of a dump closed over one hundred years ago. Waste discharge, for example from septic tanks, and the location of petrol stations are often included. As you can imagine, most country houses are not connected to the mains sewer and have a septic tank or cesspit. Your environmental search, therefore, may have a long list of sewage outflows that are simply domestic and unlikely to form any significant hazard, especially if the tanks have been upgraded, which will become enforceable in 2020 (some say you can drink the water from a modern biodigester, but I would not advise testing the theory....).

The environmental search will also state the flood risk; an increasingly relevant matter in these environmentally changing times.

A separate search can be obtained for Japanese knotweed, but will not necessarily be very accurate as only reported outbreaks will be included. This is currently a big concern as the associated risk of damage has been somewhat overstated and most lenders are restricting lending on houses with this invasive species, therefore creating unnecessary difficulties with marketing and value.

Water authority searches

A water authority search will establish where your water comes from (not necessarily from the mains, I have looked at houses that have a private supply from a borehole), and whether there are any public drains on the property. A public sewer on the site could impact your ability to extend a house.

Additional Recommended searches.

Here are a few other searches that should be considered depending on the circumstances and location.

Mining Search

There are numerous mines throughout the country, not just the mining hot spots in Wales and the west country, but also in some quite unexpected areas, for example, Kent. Depending on the area where you are buying a property, a mining search should be carried out to establish whether the home you want might be about to fall down a mine shaft. In fact that is virtually impossible, but a bit of subsidence on unstable ground caused by an old mine is not uncommon.

Chancel Repair Liability search

In certain areas, a home owner could be liable for the cost of repairs to a parish church. This is known as a chancel repair. Under chancel repair liability, homeowners living within the parishes of churches built on or before 1536 can be held liable for church repair costs. The law dates back to the time of Henry VIII. A property may be some distance from a church and still be affected.

Following a law change in October 2013, the church must now establish and lodge their right to claim repair costs from liable home owners with the Land Registry, but in certain circumstances the church can still insist a property owner is liable for repairs even if the liability hasn't been registered. In reality, while potentially thousands of houses in England are at risk, claims are exceptionally rare. There is, however, case law that supports the church and the risk, although slight, can devalue a home by several thousand pounds. A chancel repair search only costs a few pounds but in my view is essential. Chancel repair insurance is available and seems cheap, but is a license to print money for the insurers, not least because it is heavily caveated. In fact, if insurance is already in place, make sure your solicitor explains the caveats and potential shortcomings; another good reason to engage a decent conveyancer.

Check the House is not a Pup – Also known as Getting a Survey

Of all the processes you need to go through when buying a property, getting a mortgage, employing a solicitor etc. perhaps of the most important, yet often overlooked, is the survey. Getting a survey to check the condition of the place you are buying is not obligatory. It astounds me, however, how many people choose not to do so simply because of the extra cost. If ever there was a false economy then this is it. You are making probably the biggest purchase of your life, surely you need to check if you are in for any major expense for unexpected repairs?

You cannot try out a house first (although I did meet someone recently who rented a holiday home that was for sale before they bought it. Clever idea, but not an option 99.9% of the time).

Having a survey is very much like asking the AA (other car rescue companies are available….) to test drive your car if you are not available to do it yourself.

Often I am asked if it is really worth having a survey done? Some people tell me point-blank that they are a waste of money. Believe me, I know many buyers who have been badly burned by this attitude.

The following case is a very recent scenario that arose at my practice. We had an enquiry from a prospective client who was buying a small recently refurbished converted flat in a Victorian terrace. The chap explained that the outside of the building had been very well maintained, and the interior completely re-plumbed rewired and refitted. He was unsure whether it was worth proceeding with the survey. We explained that there may well be deficiencies that he hasn't spotted, we are experts in this field and inevitably would always recommend someone pays the few extra pounds required for a survey when spending several hundred thousand. Even if we found nothing wrong, at least there would be peace of mind.

The buyer considered and decided to engage our services. This is what we discovered.......

The flat had just one bedroom and one bathroom. The toilet was connected to a macerator. Ok skip the next bit if squeamish…. a macerator is used when there is no practical means of installing a traditional gravity waste pipe. It mashes up the waste and pumps it through a thin pipe.

There were two serious problems with this particular installation. Firstly, a macerator does not meet building regulation requirements if it is the only toilet in the home. So if it breaks down, or there is a power cut, get out the potty.

The second difficulty was the plumbing. The pipe connecting to the toilet extended upward through the roof into the rear. Nothing wrong with this. It is meant to be a continuous pipe without joints. In this case, not only was this the wrong sort of pipe, but one of the joints was simply with a blob of silicon. Under pressure from the pumped waste, it is quite likely that at any time that joint could pop and anyone in the bedroom underneath would be in for an extremely unpleasant surprise......

Needless to say there was nothing else wrong with the flat. However, to meet building regulations the bathroom had to be relocated to the back of the building completely changing the configuration of the flat. A very close call for our clients, who needless to say did not proceed with the purchase.

On another occasion, we inspected a lovely refurbished period listed building, you know the chocolate box scenario I referred to before? One of those.

Although generally in excellent condition, we discovered that the frame supporting the incredibly heavy stone roof was resting on just one thin post which was buckling under the weight. Eventually that post will snap and the roof structure could come crashing down. The purchaser managed to negotiate a reduction in the price to reflect the cost of strengthening the roof. Unfortunately for other reasons the sale later fell through and we understand the eventual purchaser went ahead without having a survey. Perhaps they were shown our report. If not, I just hope that the defect was revealed to them or had been repaired before the property was put back on the market.

So the expression 'it's stood for 500 years, it will be fine!' does not always apply. It will not necessarily stand for another 500. In fact many of the old period properties built all those years ago did collapse, and the materials were often salvaged and used elsewhere. If they had built them properly, there would probably be plenty more lovely cottages around.

Problems are not uncommon in modern property. Windows get installed incorrectly, plumbing is often shoddy, and there are usually numerous snags outstanding in new builds.

Yes a survey is an additional cost, but it is absolutely value for money. No matter the age of the property or how tight your funds are, *get a survey.*

Choosing the right Survey - and the right Surveyor

There are three types of inspection carried out by surveyors; the mortgage valuation (often mistakenly called 'a survey', even by many in the industry, a 'Homebuyer Survey, and a Building Survey, once called a structural survey and still sometimes referred to as such.

The survey types are often referred to as a Scheme 1,2 and 3.

The Mortgage Valuation

If you're getting a mortgage, the bank will send a valuer to the house to assess the value of the property. This is to check they are not lending you too much money in relation to the value of the house. For example, if you are paying £200,000 for a house, and they are prepared to lend you up to 80%, in principle, they will lend you £160,000. Sometimes the valuer will tell the bank that the property, in their opinion, is worth just say £180,000. The bank, therefore, will lend just 80% of £180,000, i.e. just £144,000. You can imagine the chaos this causes in the transaction and the chain.

You cannot nominate the valuer, as this will be regarded as a conflict of interest.

If you are purchasing a relatively straightforward property, for example a three bed semi, for a reasonably small additional fee you can upgrade the mortgage valuation to a more detailed report. The RICS describe this as a Homebuyer Survey. This means the mortgage valuer will spend not just a few minutes at the house, but probably at least an hour or longer to carry out more detailed analysis of the condition. The Homebuyer survey format used by mortgage valuers is produced by the RICS with, in my opinion, a slightly irritating traffic light system, i.e. red for danger. Some surveyors (including us) produce their own format. Ours is bespoke with photographs. As we do not carry out mortgage valuations, you would have to pay extra for this stand-alone report that is independent of the valuation. Sometimes however it is worth investing the additional fee as defects found will not be cross referenced back to the valuation report potentially giving rise to a mortgage retention.

A retention is where you are offered a mortgage but a sum is withheld to reflect works that, in the opinion of the mortgage valuer, should be addressed to protect the lender's security. The retention is released only when the works are completed. Alleged dampness is a most common cause for mortgage retentions. I use the word alleged as damp is often misdiagnosed, causing unnecessary disturbance and building costs.

The final option is the full building survey. This is literally the inspection with all the whistles and bells. You really should have a building survey of your buying a period property especially if the property is listed. A well-written building survey will not only reflect works required, but will also explain how your building should be managed; a house that is several hundred years old should be maintained holistically. Often surveyors will talk about ventilation and breathability, lime mortars instead of common cement etc.

A fourth option – a listed building survey – is a building survey with some extra checks on matters relating to these protected buildings. The surveyor will check not only the condition of the building, but also advise the client of any potential non-conformant changes made.

As a rule surveyors will not test the services (i.e. the electrics, heating etc.), but should have sufficient knowledge to tell you whether these installations are suspect and dated simply from a visual inspection. Provided power and water has not been disconnected, they will be able to run the sanitary fittings, heating etc.

If these installations are in the opinion of the surveyor reasonably modern, simply asking for a gas safe certificate and the service record is often sufficient.

Drain sometimes should be tested especially if they run under the house but again the surveyor will usually lift the manholes and flush the loos to check there is a clear flow. This will not however necessarily be the case if you go for the briefer homebuyer report, and especially if you simply rely on the mortgage valuation; don't expect any comment whatsoever on these installations.

Modern, especially upmarket homes have increasingly complex services. Under-floor heating is commonplace, mood lighting, centralised lighting systems, green energies such as solar and PV (photovoltaic) panels, ground and air source heat pumps are becoming ever more popular. The rise of the mobile app means many of these systems can be controlled by your device quite literally from the opposite side of the world. Although surveyors should have a full understanding of these installations, they will not necessarily be able tell you how well they are working. This really will require more detailed examination by specialists and I would strongly recommend you arrange a test if you are buying a house with these complex facilities, as they can often go wrong and are sometimes incorrectly installed.

Inevitably no house is perfect. If you are buying an older property, the surveyor is bound to raise a number of issues. Mostly these would be typical and if you're freaked out by slight damp or wobbly walls, a chat with the surveyor should put your mind at rest. If you are still concerned then perhaps an older house is not for you. Every now and then however the surveyor will find something that is a genuine concern. For example a dodgy roof, an unsupported chimneybreast, dry rot etc.

Ultimately any defect can be resolved but obviously money is usually required and it would not be unreasonable to go back to the vendors and asked for a reduction in the agreed price.

Choosing the Surveyor

Few people outside the Chartered Surveying profession realise just how many specialities there are in the field. The following words are just a few that precede the word 'surveyor', and most have some relationship with Royal Institution of Chartered Surveyors; marine, chattel, party wall, commercial, land, quantity, valuation, estates, general practice, to name just a few. For any 'A' level student stuck for a career, there may well be one of interest for you here. However, the type a home purchaser needs in is the Residential or Building Surveyor. The latter is best suited to the really complex property. Superseding that, however, is experience. In fact, an experienced building surveyor practicing in the residential field does not necessarily even need to be a member of the RICS.

If you are buying a period property, you will want reassurance and solutions. An experienced residential building surveyor that specialises in period property is the perfect fit, but is increasingly difficult to find; many are retiring, and the younger generation often gravitate to the commercial field. There are however still a few of us alive and kicking ....

Chapter Summary

- When choosing a lawyer, do not be driven by fee – experience and good communication is the key.
- Searches take time and should be put in hand immediately
- Always get a survey, preferably from a surveyor independent of the mortgage lender.
- A mortgage valuation is not a survey.
- Choose a surveyor with experience of the type of house you are buying.

CHAPTER 9

When Things Go Wrong.

It is a sad but well-known fact that the home buying process in the British market, certainly outside Scotland, is protracted and fraught with obstacles. Finding a buyer that is willing to proceed at an acceptable price is usually straightforward provided you follow the guidelines in this book. After that, you are in the hands of the gods and regrettably fall throughs are commonplace. The bigger the chain, the greater the risk as it just takes one chink to create a Jenga like collapse.

There are countless causes for a fall through. A below purchase price valuation by the mortgage valuer meaning the buyer cannot proceed at the agreed price, mortgage companies withdrawing mortgage offers (common place in the financial crisis but less so today), an adverse survey, the solicitor reporting deficiencies for example in the property title or lease, job loss, relocation, illness, death, pregnancy, divorce, and so on.

Sometimes, a buyer simply has a change of heart and decides they don't want to move after all. Usually the reason given will be a spurious excuse, especially if costs have already been incurred. An adverse survey is often cited in these instances, which is rather annoying for us surveyors as we do not want to be blamed for fall throughs unless there is a serious problem with the building.

So what can you do to reduce the risk? Probably the most effective steps are to do everything in your power to speed up the process; the less time between offer and completion, the less risk of a fall through. So do use a responsive solicitor (another good reason not to choose the cheapest option), call your solicitor and the estate agents on all sides to ask for updates and to see if anyone needs chasing, you could even hand deliver some documents on behalf of parties, and avoid being one of the causes of delays. For example, make sure you complete and send all documents as soon as possible, including mortgage forms, sellers packs etc.

Perhaps the only other advice I can give you is to hold tight, and don't get too excited until you have exchanged contracts. On the plus side, even after a fall through, invariably another buyer will appear and eventually something will stick.

Also, you might want to avoid getting too friendly with the buyer, especially if they are local, as you will no doubt meet in the street at some time in the future, which is fine, provided they did go ahead with the purchase, but could end in tears if they did not!

The absolute ideal is to avoid a lengthy chain. The holy grail is to find a cash buyer who is not reliant on an extended chain. As a buyer, a vacant house is the preferred option; the seller usually *needs* to sell and wont suddenly change their mind. The chances are, however, that you will end up with neither. Sometimes it is worth accepting a lower offer from somebody in a stronger position, but usually, you just have to grit your teeth and accept there might be several ducks to get in a row before the chain is ready for exchange.

Chapter Summary

- Sale fall throughs are common, but usually just a temporary setback.
- To reduce the risk of sales falling through, do everything you can to speed up the process.
- The highest offers are not always the strongest.
- Avoid lengthy chains if possible.

CHAPTER **10**

Signing Along the Dotted Line - Exchange of Contracts and Completion.

Toward the end of the hopefully not too tortuous conveyancing process, there will be mutterings about 'exchange and completion dates'. So what are these, and what is the difference between them?

Exchange of contracts and Paying Deposits

When all the ducks *are* finally in a row, contracts, that your solicitor will have asked you to sign in advance, can be exchanged. In reality, the solicitors do not actually meet with the other party to swap contracts and shake hands. This is really just a phone call. At the point of exchange, the date for completion is set, which is usually two or three weeks, depending on circumstances. Once exchange has been carried out, there is no turning back unless you're prepared to lose a substantial sum of money. When you exchange, you must pay a deposit towards the purchase. The usual amount is 10%, but with the agreement of the vendor can be lower depending on the circumstances of the individual purchaser. The lower the percentage, the greater the trust put into the buyer.

Some buyers are not aware or perhaps have forgotten since the last time they purchased that they need to deposit money on exchange of contracts before they sell their home, and may not have this sum available. If the purchase price is relatively high, which in London and the south is invariably the case, 10% is a considerably sum of money. For example if you are buying a house for say £500,000, you need to find £50,000. This money goes towards protecting others in the chain from expenses incurred if you break the contract and withdraw after contracts have been exchanged.

If you are a first time buyer with a 95% mortgage, then the chances are you will not have 10% of the purchase price to spare, but probably just the 5% difference between the mortgage level and the purchase price, i.e. plus an amount to cover the various fees. Unless the vendor is prepared to accept this lower deposit, you will need to find the additional £15,000 from somewhere, for example the bank of Mum and Dad or from alternative savings. If you are a second time buyer, all your equity might be tied up in the house.

There is a potential saviour; if you are buying and selling, your solicitor can usually use your buyer's deposit in connection with your purchase so you may not have to find any deposit monies at all, or at least not the entire deposit. Also, as you may be paying stamp duty on completion, this amount can contribute to deposit monies and simply transferred to the government coffers on completion. A first time buyer however does not usually need to pay stamp duty, so this money might not be available.

Even if the deposit is reduced to 5%, there is a high possibility that you will be legally obliged to pay 10% of the potential purchase price if you renege on the deal once contracts have been exchanged. So whatever you do, do not exchange contracts without being 100% certain that everything is ready, i.e. you have all the money to purchase through whatever means, be it for cash, with a mortgage, bridging loan etc. Your conveyancer will ensure that this is the case so the likelihood of a shortfall is extremely remote. If you are self-conveyancing (ill advised!), then absolutely make sure you are ready; do not let emotions get in the way of the real deal. Even if you are confident the money will be available by the time completion is due, if it is not in place now, do not exchange contracts.

Between exchange and completion

So why are there two separate deals, i.e. the exchange of contracts, and completion?

Unless you're a first-time buyer and purchasing a property that is empty, you need time to confirm removal dates, pack, redirect mail, close utility accounts and so on etc.

The period between exchange of contracts, when you are totally committed, and completion, i.e., the moment the home is yours is usually a minimum of two weeks but on occasion can be as much as six months, if for example a purchaser is abroad and not returning for some time, and the vendor is agreeable for their own reasons, perhaps still looking for a house to buy or rent.

At the other extreme, exchange and completion can happen at the same time. This might be a sale from one investor to another where a tenant remains in place, or for example if there are joint owners and one is selling their share to the other. Same day exchange and completion was quite common in London when the market was booming and sellers were demanding completion within just a few days of the offer; a bit of a nightmare for all the professionals involved. On many occasion we have had to drop everything to inspect a house in town and report back within 24hrs. Not easy; us surveyors like time to reflect.

For most people, however, the period between exchange of contracts, when you are totally committed, and completion, i.e., the moment the home is yours (deep breath), is a time for action and can be a little frantic.

These are the steps you should take between exchange and completion.

Get your new home insured.

Of course anyone that owns a building should insure it. However, not everyone realises that from the point of exchange, as the buyer you become responsible for insuring the property, even though technically you do not yet own it. This is vital as you are now contracted to buy it, and if the sellers have inadequate cover, or worst still, no insurance at all, and the property becomes damaged, you may end up paying the full price for a property that has burned to the ground.

In fact a very good friend had this unlucky experience. Thankfully no one was hurt and insurance was in place (she was a solicitor so all boxes were ticked). In fact it worked in their favour; the insurance covered temporary accommodation and storage costs, a new kitchen and new decorations throughout to boot (don't go getting any ideas now, or your new home could be somewhere very different with bars across the windows…..). It was, however, a very horrible experience for the elderly couple that owned the house.

Building insurance will cover against most usual risks; subsidence, fire, flood etc. It does not cover contents (carpets for example), you need separate cover for that.

Like any insurance, the premium and excess will rise with the risk. In areas of clay subsoils which shrink during prolonged dry weather, the excess for subsidence claims can be as much as £5,000. In some areas, it is not possible to get insurance for flood damage at all if the property is, for example, in a flood plain, or there is a history of persistent problems (this is a very different to the flood caused when your teenager leaves the bath running and goes out for the night, which will be covered, unless of course they did it on purpose……).

It is vital the insured sum is sufficient; if you are under insured, the insurance company will only pay for a proportion of any loss. For example, if the actual cost to demolish and rebuild the property is say £250,000, but you only have cover for half that amount, i.e. £125,000, the insurers will only pay for 50% of a successful claim. So if there is a fire that causes £10,000 of damage, the insurer will pay only £5,000. This is called averaging.

If in doubt you should ask a surveyor to calculate the sum insured for you, especially if the building is unusual or listed, which can triple the cost of repairs as damaged fine details such as ornate ceilings must be replicated.

If you are buying a leasehold property, usually the managing agents and/or freeholder are responsible for insuring the building. You should however, ask for details as the cover might be inadequate.

Packing and removals

Some people start packing in preparation for the move way before exchange of contracts. Others do nothing as they do not want to tempt fate. My advice is simple; the more you have, the sooner you should declutter and pack. If you have lived in the same home for 40 years, the challenge can seem insurmountable but if you make an early start, you will soon see light at the end of the tunnel.

In fact, like most people you probably need a jolly good declutter anyway, and even if the move is delayed or does not happen at all, there is never a bad time for a cathartic clear out. We have a clear out every summer. I have no idea where everything comes from.

If you find a buyer really quickly, you will be grateful you started the clear out well in advance; on many occasion I have heard people in panic saying, '*it's all happened so quickly!*', while I am thinking, '*I told you so....*'.

In fact, if you have followed my advice from earlier in the book, you will already have cleared the decks to improve the saleability of your home. This will also make your removal costs cheaper. If you get quotes from the removal company and they cannot see the wood for the trees, they will quote high to cover themselves.

Incidentally, ideally you should get your removal quotes and dates pencilled in before exchange; they can get booked up and the last thing you need is to do the removal work yourself, even if you are just going around the corner. It is fine if you have few belongings (like first time buyers with just a mattress, or the divorced man left with nothing but the hi-fi and his Harley Davison), but if it is a typical family move, you will completely underestimate how much work is involved. I speak from experience; the one occasion I moved myself was both horribly time consuming and back breaking work - never again. Removal costs are surprisingly reasonable and worth every penny, it is a competitive field and they will even package everything up for safety. They also have insurance, which you don't if you move yourself.

Completion

Completion is quite literally when the deal is finally done - the magic moment when your solicitor tells you purchase monies have been transferred and you are handed the key to your new home! Usually the key is handed to the estate agent and you can go along and pick it up from them.

For obvious reasons, they will be as happy as you are.

Chapter Summary

- Make sure you have enough funds for the deposit.
- Ensure there is sufficient time for you to arrange the move and pack between exchange of contracts and completion.

- You will need to insure the home you are buying when you exchange contracts, not when you complete the purchase.

- If you are downsizing and have a huge amount of 'stuff', start the clear out even before you exchange.

- Get removal quotes and dates pencilled in before exchange.

CHAPTER 11

Over the Threshold

They say the best things in life are free. They are often the briefest too. This is by far the most enjoyable, and inevitably the briefest chapter.

If, while reading this book, you have been working your way through the sale and purchase of a property then you have probably experienced a host of emotions; distress, annoyance, frustration, excitement, disappointment, but hopefully this book has eased the process.

If you are a first time buyer, then you have achieved the goal that most of the British population strive for, you now own your own home.

If you previously rented, you no longer run the risk of being forced to move by a landlord. You can paint the walls bright pink with orange spots, and in fact carry out any improvements you like (unless of course the building is listed, then you have that pernickety conservation officer to deal with).

If you have moved for the first time in many years, you too have a new adventure ahead.

So congratulations, you made it, you have overcome the fear.

In fact, you may well be moving many more times, especially during the early part of your working and family life.

So don't sit on your laurels, get ready for the next step and check out those property portals..............

Lightning Source UK Ltd.
Milton Keynes UK
UKHW021832140621
385513UK00008B/138

9 781802 270419